BLACK SWAN

Pitt Poetry Series

Ed Ochester, Editor

LYRAE VAN CLIEF-STEFANON

BLACK SWAN

University of Pittsburgh Press

The publication of this book is supported by a grant
from the Pennsylvania Council on the Arts.

Published by the University of Pittsburgh Press, Pittsburgh, Pa., 15260
Copyright © 2002, Lyrae Van Clief-Stefanon
All rights reserved
Manufactured in the United States of America
Printed on acid-free paper
10 9 8 7 6 5 4 3 2 1
ISBN 0-8229-5787-6

This book is the winner of the 2001 Cave Canem Poetry Prize,
chosen by Marilyn Nelson. The prize is awarded annually by
Cave Canem Foundation, Inc., to the best manuscript by an
African American poet who has not yet published a full-length
book of poems.

for Justin

. . . good times,

bad times,

any time. . . .

CONTENTS

I

II

III

LEDA

for my mother

Imagine Leda black—
skinny legs   peach-switch
scarred   vaselined to gleaming
like magnolia leaves   Imagine
a teenager   hips asway like moss
switchin' down a dirt road
Florida orange blossom
water behind her ears
her tight sheath-skirt
azalea pink
A freemason Pentecostal
preacher's child
sent down from the city
to be raised by her grandmama
A girl   assured her whole life
I never asked for you no-how!
I asked for your sister.
Imagine
the god/swan's neck
draped around her neck
like a white down noose
For years she walked straight
home from school   past tempting
crescent lakes   warned off
from sweet patches
of sugarcane
because of the snakes
and the gators

3

199 LEE STREET

Where the macramé owl,
dirty-white, fuzzing from rain,
with darkly surprised wood-knob eyes,
must have hung on the porch
til its ropes rotted,
where toad holes pocked
the front yard and I wrenched
the cool damp faucet, a metal flower,
drove the green hose deep
to flood them out,
I stripped bark from trees in fat bands
down to the meat,
green-rimmed like melon rind
and ultra-white, new wounds
I licked to taste the bitter.
An old address sings girlhood
when mosquito bites warned evening
and I marked their flat mounds
with fingernail x's, crickets scratched out
their first sharp notes, lost
in the house where I learned the red rug
against my chest, my knees
my tongue, and the back room's
stark patterned tile—
blue red blue white red blue—
and the scrape of the unplaned back door
and the sound of the tight fit
and the final hard clink of its frosted glass slats
disturbed, then shaken into place.

HOME: *VOLUSIA COUNTY, FLORIDA*

This is a place that I can say I left.
The cesspool, choking shit into the tub,
backed up. The heat. The way the ground could shift,

could swallow! Sinkholes sucking down the heft
of house to abscess, memory to hub
for shafts of fear and prayer. This is I left:

The threat of family, the way love cleft
my tongue, the faith I'd teach myself to stub
out like a burning soul. The ground could shift

and churn itself to glass, glittering, deft.
The grit of home between my teeth, I grub
to find what's shining, dig through what is left

chipped, broken, archeology a gift.
Undaunted, I unearth my life, then dub
myself scientist as I label, sift.

With this salvage, how can I be bereft?
Lift each artifact from its grid and rub
the dirt off gently. See how ruins shift.
This is a place that I can say I left.

EYE

When I scratched the screen a lizard
the green of spring leaves skittered
underneath the azalea hedge.
Its skin turned mulch brown.
I pressed my nose against the door and stared.
I stared until the screen's gray mesh
rose three-dimensional around my face.
It seemed I put my hand through
what I touched. Beyond the screen, Florida sky
stretched wide and flat like a blue sheet on the line.

When storms bunched up a gray stripe
spread across the lawn, creeping shade
a line crossing sidewalks and grass.
Fat raindrops popped off the front step
until the screen's damp metal smelled like ozone and loam
and I fell asleep in the doorway.
When I woke I found the sky crocheted
yellow-green and tucked tight around everything
and changing. I filled the fine wire squares
with panes of water too small to see through.

DINAH

And Dinah the daughter of Leah
which she bare unto Jacob, went out
to see the daughters of the land.

Genesis **34:1**

I grew up watching them cut their eyes,
grit their teeth at each other.
My aunt entering a room
stiffened my mother. They warred
years over that old man
asleep in the back room—
my father, spent.

Their weapons: sons
they pushed from their bodies.
My mother bore six,
prayed with each *Now*
he will not hate me. He
will not wipe himself
with the sheet, leave
my bed without looking
back. Tonight,
when he comes he will
not picture my sister.
I never played with girls,

only this army
of brothers they mustered
feeding my father female
bodies, other women snatched
into his bed, delivered
like sacrifices. They consumed
themselves, wasteful, greedy.
When I went

7

out into the city
that day I wanted to meet
women who looked
at each other,
whose bodies kept
their softness in
the presence of their sisters.
Instead, I met a man,
relearned
my family's definitions
for love, body, weapon.

EIGHT

Smiling, he says *I know you like me girl*
and tries to coax me down onto the bed.
He slides his middle finger round the edge
of my blue shorts. I don't know if I should
shoot a bird at him, shoot him dead. At eight
what I know is Mama keeps bullets in
the bottom dresser drawer of this same room,
but I have never seen the gun. He smirks
Don't even know what pussy is, do you?
I know more than I want to know. I smile,
and draw him to the game of war my brothers
fight with pillows against his sisters while
our mothers, off at prayer meeting for hours,
praise God. I've learned to call on other powers.

PERIOD

for Judy Blume

I wanted blood.
I called *Are You There, God?*
It's Me, Margaret, read the words like
psalms, knew them like the lines
in my open palm. I read
the boys' version too,
the one about wet dreams,
its title no prayer, no supplication,
only the indecision that expresses
agency, engorged with
options. I understood
not one word of it,
the workings of
their foreign bodies, grown
before I tried to reason why
my brother might have been
touching me. I wanted blood
just like those white girls
praying for it:
so normal and so blessed,
them and their bleeding.

DAPHNE

Fear glistened
In the sweat
On my skin
Until it dried
And cracked
And darkened
My *Father,*
Save me!
Hovered
In humid air
Hung there until
The brown bark
Of prayer
Encased me
This is
What passes
For safety
Now stillness
Settles on me
Like long vines
And silence
Entwines me
Rooted
Mute.

ROADSIDE STAND

❦

The man on the side of the road sells watermelons.
Split fruit sweats in the Florida heat.
I will watch men's hands my whole life.
With a dirty jagged nail he flicks away a black seed.

❦

Split fruit sweats in the Florida heat.
Sun like an orange cut, dripping, slick.
With a dirty nail he flicks away a black seed.
The day's too sticky for melons' damp sweet smell.

❦

Sliced orange sun drips humid, slick.
All I want is tomatoes for supper
this day's too sticky for sickly sweet melon smell.
Five red tomatoes, stacked in a small basket,

❦

All I want is these tomatoes. Mama says,
You know your brothers will want a hot meal.
Five tomatoes sit stacked, pretty in a small basket.
At home she cooks rice until the walls sweat.

❦

Mama knows my brothers will want a hot meal.
House too hot to stand, but the boys are happy.
She steams rice until the walls sweat.
And pulls out photo albums after dinner.

❦

House too hot to stand but the boys are happy.
In the baby picture I am fat as a turkey.
Mama holds the album open on her lap.
Everybody has pictures just like this.

⚘

In the picture I'm naked, plump as a turkey.
I am on my back, fat legs splayed open.
Everybody has pictures just like this.
I huddle in close to Mama.

⚘

Baby in the picture's fat legs cocked open.
With her index finger Mama points to my vagina.
I huddle in close to her with my brothers.
She makes a low disapproving noise, mocking.

⚘

She points to my vagina with her index finger.
My brothers learn my body is this wordless, dirty joke.
Mama makes a low disapproving noise, mocking.
Watch me learn shame.

⚘

My brother learns my body, this wordless, dirty joke
on the back room's thick, blood red carpet.
Watch me learn shame. Watch me learn shame.
Why do I keep getting stuck here?

⚘

On the back room's thick, blood red carpet
Think about those five tomatoes, sliced with salt and pepper.
Why do I keep getting stuck here?
Five ripe tomatoes on a clean plate.

⚘

13

Think of fresh tomatoes sliced with salt and pepper.
The man on the side of the road sells watermelons
and vine ripe tomatoes waiting for a clean plate.
I will watch men's hands my whole life.

TAMAR'S BLUES

> And Tamar put ashes on her head,
> and rent her garment of divers colors that was on her,
> and laid her hand on her head,
> and went on crying. So Tamar remained
> desolate in her brother Absalom's house.
>
> *II Samuel* 13:19, 20

I used to wear purple and turquoise.
I used to wear sienna and maroon.
I used to wear silver.
I used to worship the ground my brothers walked.
I used to believe my father loved me.
I used to answer when anyone called.

Where shall I cause my shame to go?
Where shall I cause my shame to go?
How can I remain in this house?
How can I leave?

On the roof he is fucking my father's wives.
On the roof he is fucking them, ten in a row.
He is making a marathon of semen.
He is pulling a train on himself.

I imagine the tents visible from miles away,
canvas whipping hot air like something to prove.
He is pulling a train on himself, my brother.
He is drawing a crowd.

Where shall I cause my shame to go?
Where shall I cause my shame to go?
This is not even my story any more.
This has never been about me.

II

GETTING SAVED

Dust shouted into the air during testimony service
hangs in the hazy church like the mantle of the spirit. Trembling
I open my eyes, my mouth still moving *Jesus, Jesus*

Jesus standing in the same spot where my sister
got saved years ago, her pleas high-pitched, panicked,
accelerating until the name became undecipherable.

Mother Johnson, Mother Mitchell, Mother Brown surround me.
Mother Murphy whispers her mouth against my ear
Say Jesus, honey. Tha's it.

Jesus filling my head like they say my husband's
I love you will someday fill me
when I'm in my bed, out my bedclothes.

Outside, parked beneath the glow of stained glass
the children of the saints fuck, fog the windows of deacons' cars.
I close my eyes with the thought

my stomach tightening. The circle of mothers
urgent in prayer rub my back, pat sweat from my face
with their embroidered handkerchiefs.

Last month Mother Murphy's daughter led
the youth choir in a chorus and fainted before the pulpit.
Drunk in the Spirit Pastor calls it

when you can feel the colors swirling: the red
of pulpit-seat velvet, the pews' dark stain,
the congregation's various browns in feverish

seizures of salvation. Robin Murphy's starting to show.
One meetin' baby born last week; hers makes three more
on the way. The mothers fan me

with their funeral home fans, sing *Jesus,*
coming through, *Jesus.*
I squinch my eyes hard so I can open one unnoticed.

The undercurrent of imminent shouting
runs through the church.
I must be saved, I think. I must be saved.

DANAE

i been thirsty so long that my mouth feels
like parchment / got words written cross it

Patricia Jones

1. Brass Room

I spray paint every piece of brass
flat black: glass-topped coffee table,
bedside lamps with their silk
green shades. I know my father
decorated this room to punish me.
I tape off marble bathroom tile
with brown paper
and spray tub fixtures:
faucet and handles. I cover
the floor and paint
the brass clawed feet.
There is nothing I can do
about the walls, this hammered metal
glint distorting reflection.
I glimpse myself knowing no man
will ever twist open
these doors. There is no use for
so much shining.

2. *Shower of Gold*

Water spills over my ankles
as the tub fills. I imagine
the faucet's gleaming throat,
its valves wide open.
I close my eyes and pray,
the gold behind my eyelids
from the skylight
deliquescent. Taste God
in acrid bitter tears;
a piss-warm stream
I recognize as love.

MAGNIFICAT

In the pulpit, in the swirling dust after
the saints have sung "Sweeping through the City"
and the front pew's children danced,
stomping towards the altar their cadenced
hoedown, holiest of double-Dutch

Pentecostal, pastor opens his mouth.
How quietly Mary's speech falls past
the neat square patch of hair beneath his lips, *He
that is mighty has done to me great things,
and holy is His name.* His belly pushes

against the buttons of his three-piece
suit's black vest and I almost would
believe in the quiet hum
of "Come to Jesus," of every saint's
sweet supplication. How many times

would a girl hush the hop-skipped
rhythm of pulse, lie back
in sacrifice, take in salvation
that she can't hold. Pastor opens like
gardenia blossom every Sunday,

so meekly. He has come this far
by faith. Girl-child, I lean
into this offering,
get my lesson, make flesh
word.

PACKAGE

1.

Today it's as hot in Pennsylvania
as it must be down in Florida.
Signs on two separate churches
flash warnings.

The first—*And you think it's hot here!*
The second—*Turn or burn.*
"Hell," my new favorite song,
plays every fifteen minutes on the radio.

Stuffed into the mailbox, bulging like trash,
brown paper bound tight with clear tape,
sent from Florida book rate,
addressed in Mama's cursive.

Ripped open, reveals Wallace Stevens's collected poems,
the collected poems of Langston Hughes,
a plastic cross-stitched "Welcome" plaque,
a pink pair of panties in a little pink bag,

a gospel cassette, a fifteen-piece do-it-yourself tool kit,
all crammed into a white plastic bag, its red printing repeats
Thank You Thank You Thank You Thank You
Thank You Thank You Have a Nice Day.

Yes, I read it all.
I read the note—a three-by-five card covered
in more of Mama's cursive—though she read it to me
over the phone two weeks ago.

It says *Peter had no idea*
what the Lord was doing in washing
the feet of the disciples. Love caused him to—
even without understanding—gladly submit

himself to the act. Unwillingness to let go
of what you thought was
has trapped you in time.
I read it all,

again, the note, the plastic bag again,
the addresses on the crumpled brown paper,
again the teal "Welcome" surrounded by white
stitched hearts, the Stevens, the Hughes, the names

of the songs on the cassette—*Give Me You, Love Joy*
Peace, Speak to Me—all again,
searching for more
neat cursive script.

I flip the three-by-five card and find
Read John 13:7 NOW (Key).
But I am tired of riddles,
God's and Mama's.

2.

Today it's as hot in Pennsylvania
as it must be down in Florida.
I open windows,
flip through Hughes and Stevens, place them

next to the blue leather Bible
waiting on the shelf.
I try on the panties, hum
the song's lyric about a suit of flame.

They are three sizes too big.
I line my trash can with the plastic Thank You bag,
toss in scrap, old receipts, wait
for the weather to break. Should I mail a Thank You note?

I reorganize my cassettes,
add the gospel tape,
look up the Scripture,   debate
the wording of a note through two cool days.

I call instead,
my voice as stiff as something shipped
as polite as Mama's.

3.

The cadence of my mother's christianese
rings through telephone wire,
defies time. I crawl into my own mouth

for fire
of tongues, for language
so perfect I cannot
understand. I find questions

clicking against the back of my teeth.
Don't you want to know
what the scripture said?
I have tossed it

into the sea
of forgetfulness. I only know
Mama must be   God   She is
so mysterious.

BROTHER

Thirteen hours into my first visit
home in three years I'm mopping
mama's kitchen floor
when my baby brother demands *how far
up the academic food chain you plan on going
before you come home and
take care of mama?*
And in my head I been cursing him out for twenty minutes
for the grease caked on this linoleum
and the plastic bag sitting up
on the counter filled with garbage,
for quitting school anyway and moving back
into her house a grown man,
for the marine corps training book in his room
open to diagrams for hand-to-hand killing techniques
and the receipt for a tattoo of a skull
with crossed knives stabbed up through the eyes
marking the page, money gladly spent
though he begrudged me twenty dollars
to put some groceries in her house
this morning. I spit *fuck you*
and fear I've lost the last
black man in my life.

EUROPA: *DAYTONA BEACH, FLORIDA*

She is still enough to taste
standing on the beach   the town where she was born
She watches the sun   the first pip of orange-yellow
that peeks through flat blue then spreads like song
Every morning this miracle   and others   the swoop
of gulls diving   into the wave-laps for fish
or the salty dash that day   the sea turtles hatched
Today   a bull   as still as God   and tame enough
to touch

Who has not waited   spellbound
for a glimpse of God   Even now
dawn's devout dot the flat-packed sand
parked for worship   Who has not listened
for a whisper in sea spray and sunlight
prayed for a sight   like this   one beast
so wildly out of place it might speak
it might just speak   and she would be
the only witness   Before the first tide's crowd arrives
she walks towards the bull   Before the hot day's flood
of tourists   she enters his presence
Who has not been betrayed with waiting
wanting   one word   sweet
and sacred   from the mouth   of creation

What's left of her gown   twisted   around her left shoulder
whips   in the wind that catches   her hair
the smell of musk and heat   The shaft
of bull's neck   stretches   up in a taut arc
etched by rivulets of sweat   Thick veins standing

on its flanks   its great eye rolled back
With a tight grimace   it licks the sun

The muscles of her thighs   tensed high
above its haunches
she reaches   wild-eyed   for that tongue

THE DAUGHTER AND THE CONCUBINE FROM THE NINETEENTH CHAPTER OF JUDGES CONSIDER AND SPEAK THEIR MINDS

Behold, here is my daughter a maiden, and his concubine;
Them I will bring out now, and humble ye them,
And do with them what seemeth good unto you: But unto this man
Do not so vile a thing.

1.

Suddenly, I am a stranger
in my father's house.

His doors open to any man
off the street, he opens his mouth

to make me prostitute.
Pimp, he has forgotten

my name. And how I
tended his fevers, wept

at the foot of his bed, slept
prayers while age played

the fool with his body.
What thing exists too vile

for this man he's known
one half day that be

not too vile for me?
I do not need to be humbled.

1.

Last visit, I stayed four months
in my father's house.

For that, my man calls me
whore, his mouth full of bread

as this old man offers me
with his daughter

to the hoodlums in the road.
I have been whoring after home

since the day I left.
I miss my daddy's easy smile.

This time he tried so hard
to make us stay, seems like

he saw this coming.
My man can talk

so pretty when he wants to,
pretty enough

And this girl, this wayfaring
man's woman who sticks so

close to the walls seems like
she longs to slip into

her own shadow, she looks
humble down to her bones.

to love, but I know
when he looks

unsatisfied. I know
when he looks unsatisfied

not to stand staring
into a man's mouth.

But the men would not hearken to him:
So the man took his concubine, and brought her forth unto them;
And they knew her, and abused her all the night until the morning:
And when the day began to spring, they let her go.

2.

They would have gone.
They would have heckled the
    house,
cursed and called until they'd
    grown

bored. They might have thrown
a stone, broken a window, but
    then
they would have gone

and left us alone.
But he brought her to them
the way one might drop

an ant into a spider's web.

2.

I never learned but one prayer
that was Daddy
And Daddy was answer
quick to answer
And Daddy and me were praise
And Daddy was Hallelujah
And I was Glory Glory
And Daddy was Great
Day in the Morning
And I was Yes Lord Yes
And I was a gift once
And I was Daddy's to give
And Daddy was joy and sorrow
And Daddy was Oh
my baby gal done got big
And Daddy was Lord

And my father, silent, watched
curious to see destruction.

It could have easily been me.
It could have easily been me.
It could have easily been me.

Not one creature stirs.
It is as though the birds
no longer recognize

morning: a cheap faint glow
haunting the eastern sky
and what is there to sing about?

If I had but a burrow
I would call myself blessed.
If I had a grave, I would climb
   into it.

she done grown and gone
And Daddy said
Make that negro treat you right
And Daddy said Come back if he
   don't
And Daddy said Come anyway
I'm making your favorite
And Daddy said Come anyway
Y'all can have your old room but
I am in the eye of something so
   bright
I am in the middle of light
I am in the middle of something
   so
bright I can't see day
breaking I am in the middle of
something so bright Daddy
I'm praying for night

Then came the woman in the dawning of the day,
And fell down at the door of the man's house
Where her lord was, till it was light.

3.

The smell of death squats
in every corner: this house stinks
of men. I have to spit.
My mouth keeps
filling with saliva. In the kitchen
I hold the back of my hand
to my nose

3.

Day comes like something
snatched from me
I keep
hearing snatches, songs
Precious Lord,
take my hand
the same line keeps

and try to remember
some other
smell than male
sweat and musk
and spilled semen
that hangs heavy
in these rooms. I am afraid
to open the windows,
afraid the outside air
will carry the same
smell,
will add to this mixture
blood.

catching me
I am tired
I am tired
I am tired
Do not lead me
to the light
I am afraid
of what waits for me
Precious Lord,
where is my
Lord
I am
tired

And her lord rose up in the morning,
And opened the doors of the house, and went out to go his way:
And, behold, the woman his concubine was fallen down
At the door of the house, and her hands were upon the threshold.

4.

Ground glass.
Nightshade.
Pot ash.

Blood tired, blood
tired. Blood tired.

Polk berry.
Jimson weed.
Snake venom.

My father.
My God.

4.

Say one
sweet word
to me.

I am waiting
to be comforted.

Something
pretty
to the skin,

the dirt
beneath my fingernails,

Arsenic.   to my mouth,
Diffenbachia.   twisted and full
Monkshood.   of sand,

Blood tired. Blood   pretty words
tired. Blood tired.   for bruises,

Ground glass.   for my raw throat
Nightshade.   burning. Bring flowers
Pot ash.   for me like you

My God.   used to.

And he said unto her, Up, and let us be going.
But none answered.
Then the man took her up upon an ass,
and the man rose up, and gat him unto his place.

5.   5.

Should I
refuse
to tell
this story

May I
never again
cross my
father's
threshold

And when he was come into his house,
He took a knife, and laid hold on his concubine,
And divided her, together with her bones . . .
Consider of it, take advice, and speak your minds.

Judges 19: 24–30

6.

6.

Blood
drips from
block
to Earth
spinning witness
mud tinted
red/black
soaked.
When
a man finds
his soul
wracked
and one
finger
points back
to *this* blood,
when
the moon
goes down
in *this*
blood,
when the sun
refuses *this*
blood, my soul
will say
Yes.

I am
not forsaken
and no
war
will silence
my bones.
This Earth
drinks
my
blood
in remembrance
and no
man
will silence it.
I have put
my story
into
my sisters'
mouths
and we
will sing
and we
will wail
and we
will shout.
Amen.

Incubus

I experienced an enthusiastic fit
long before I met him—
five minutes I writhed on that church floor
open-mouthed, heaving air.
Mama witnessed and breathed
praises to the holy ghost
when, deliverance declared, I got up
with hope of the first easy sleep in months,
hope so good I dozed as she drove home.

But the noise woke me up—
the sound of myself inhaling the night's
thick air in hungry gulps sucked across my tongue,
slurped down my throat before I could hold
my own breath. I knew—
before my heavy lids flew open shutter-quick
to see no more than the silent black road curving homeward
and Mama's hand sure on the steering wheel—
the taste of revisitation.

When I met him—
when finally a stranger's familiar kiss
awakened me again,
I made love to him without so much
as an introduction.
Instead we searched for ruins
which seemed to have disappeared
after hundreds of years, overnight.
I ignored heavy-handed clues
for the thrill of a wet field moonlit,
and a slipping that didn't feel soul-first
at the time.

MYTH

In the story
first comes the cobalt
radiation:
the nurse in the iron apron;
the metal tongs handing
her the pill. In the story
first comes the Geiger counter
at her throat
tracing the pill's path.
First comes the hyperthyroid swell
of her eyes taped
closed to sleep.

She is flat-lining.
She is my mother.
She is flat-lining
and talking to
Jesus. She is pulling
at her own IV
She is dying and
bargaining:
if you let me live,
Lord, I'll praise you . . .
if you let me live,
Lord, I'll serve you . . .
if you let me live,
Lord, I'll give my life
to you and I'll thank you,
Lord, I'll thank you.

She is flat-lining.
The doctors order

a new machine.
She rises and tells them
I am going.
She hears her name
in the doctors' mouths.
They are saying
if she goes she will die.
She hears her name
in the distance
like the call for Lazarus
to come forth,
come forth. *I am*
going. I am
going she tells them.
Going home
to raise my children.

She is my mother
who walks miracle.
She is my mother
who lives faith.
She is my mother
who cries Jesus.
She is my mother
who grasps the unchanging.
She is my mother
who speaks the Word.
She is my mother
who tithes and tithes.
She is my mother
who raised her children.
She is my mother
who just died.
Rise, Mama, rise
like Lazarus.
Call on Jesus

your friend.
Please, Mama, strike
this new bargain.
Rise, Mama, rise up
again.

BOP: HAUNTING

In the evening she comes, her same unsatisfied self,
with the hard, smug look of salvation. Mama,
stop bothering me. When we argue, she says
What you're saying is not scriptural.
You need to get back in your Bible.
In one dream, I slap her. I'm tired of her mouth.

I hate to see the evening
Sun go down

Yesterday, I dreamed a vampire
held my wrist, dared me to wake
to her, corporeal, stolid. Mama,
was that you? I refused to touch
her body in the casket.
At the gravesite I refused everything
but dry-eyed silence,
her picture in my hand.

I hate to see the evening
Sun go down

This is what I get for conjuring—
Mama, after me all night,
fussing about the Holy Ghost
when what I need is sleep.
But last night I lay dreamless.
I didn't sleep sound.

I hate to see the evening
Sun go down

III

GROOVE

Facing my fear of being found wanting
in black men's eyes
meant nights of dancing.
I pressed my palms against
my partner's back,
pulled myself into his chest,
close enough
to wear my body into scar.
Slowdragging in the armory,
crowded near the deejay's stand to break
the open space
we barely moved. I followed
promise-rhythms into early morning
as though a groove meant something soft
like skin. When I slid my hands beneath his shirt
I made my body a prayer—
Please.

SPRING BOP: NEW YORK, 1999

Hold on to something, you say, arrogant
as spring: sprigs budding speckled branches
despite forecast snow. You stand beside me holding on
to nothing and I reach up too late, beat missed
smart-mouthing in my head. The subway jerks me
sideways into your always perfect timing.

Nothing but you. Nothing but you.
Nothing but you. Nothing but you.

It must be mating season
in Tompkins Square Park. One pigeon
follows another, feathers so fluffed out
it looks like it's wearing a cowl-neck sweater.
I am surrounded by the ridiculous. I am
part of it. The drums call—the steady beat
on cowbell, on the neck of a green-bottle beer—
but when they stop, no one arrives.

Nothing but you. Nothing but you.
Nothing but you. Nothing but you.

All night a false rain.
And somewhere deep
in the faucet's throat
a sound like wood block
tapped. I memorize the echo
of every day's return. Nothing new.

Nothing but you. Nothing but you.

Hum

Sometimes the hum and pull keeps me awake
all night: a low current, some faint desire—
I'll write it down. I'll see what I can make.

The next day catches me chasing the wake
of some stranger, his soapy smell—this wire
of want drawn taut. The pull keeps me awake

and searching. But to love is a mistake,
to fall for what means only to inspire,
to start the dance and see what I can make—

I'd fall in love with every man who spoke,
if not careful, of blackberries, of fire,
of turning leaves, or being kept awake

by what he couldn't name. The claim to stake
is naming. I'll change dumb awe for this dire
risk, writing, God-like, see what I can make

of longing. Wring insomnia to slake
need's lime-dry substance, take what I require.
Sometimes the hum and pull keeps me awake
all night. All night, I'll see what I can make.

LONG ROAD

This is how you know desire: bent
over a metal chair in the garden;
bent over a stairwell's iron railing; bent over
a guardrail on the highway—
the poppies planted in the median
blooming obscene pink in the overgrown grass.
And trucks at seventy miles per hour
hurtle by, whipping bits of gravel
into your calves. Your bare feet
catch slivers of green glass,
your toenails painted silver,
twinkling like change on asphalt.
The hot rubber smell of road gators:
this is how you know love. Nearby, exposed
radial wires, leftovers from a blowout.
And you feel him from behind as he leaves
the softest line of kisses
down your back. You wonder what to answer
when he whispers
do you want me to stop?
do you want me to keep loving you?

BOP: A WHISTLING WOMAN

Mama couldn't break me
of whistling like a boy the way she
stopped me hollering across streets
at boys I knew. *Let them recognize you.*
Young ladies don't raise their voices.
She knew or thought she knew
somewhere inside her, I
would not end well.

A whistling woman and a crowing hen
always come to no good end.

Let some boy use you if you want!
Her imperatives ran together. She glared,
tight-lipped at the threat of my summer days spent less
tight-legged, her fear, so ardent,
of one wrong wind, vibrating high-pitched,
passing between my lips.

A whistling woman and a crowing hen
always come to no good end.

This morning, train and teakettle catch the devil,
fifteen finches outside my kitchen window—
whose lessons do I choose?
Seven years without a slip
beneath my skirts. I'll flirt
with destruction, shame my kin.

A whistling woman and a crowing hen
always come to no good end.

STRIP

A thin brown-haired girl pouts
high on stage. She cannot swing
her slight body round the new pole.
It runs floor to ceiling, piercing
the strip club like a shaft of light
the way the voice of God appears in movies.
Except this pole is plastic and God
would gurgle because it's full of liquid
like a lava lamp. The words would have to sploosh
up through bubbles
like burps, one at a time like *Jesus.*

Is. Love. except the pole's sealed
and there is no place for love to go
so the bubbles just keep going up
and down and the girl
can't get her hands around it.
She says she misses the jungle-gym-type bar
this bubble bar replaced.
She anticipates missing the smell
of its metals on her hands after work.

Training me, she instructs *Don't touch*
your thighs. Don't touch your knees.
Keep both feet on the floor at all times.
Don't do anything I do. She smiles
at the way everything is against some law.
I go on stage and the speakers spit
out the first lines of the song I picked:
I love myself / I want you to love me.
I dance for a man. He's fifty, at least,
his wife beside him. *But you're beautiful*

she says, like a mother comforting a taunted child,
like someone else's mother. Mine said *There is nothing*
you can't talk your way out of.

The bar's dark and dollars scratch my skin.
When the next song starts I take off my bra,
my breasts covered by Florida law
with flesh brown tape. I wrap my arms,
both legs around the wide, bright pole,
spin slowly down to the floor.
Who else will pay for what he can't see?
Like God, I've always been invisible

BLACK SWAN

for Walter Wilson

I've feared the rope-thick length of neck,
the hint of wingspan, a shiver
shuffle-dealt like threat, even the orange
webbed feet, the kick
that glides him across the lake, away,
swims deep in myth, deep in what lies
in childhood to define, to overpower.

I cannot answer what difference
this color makes, this dark lack
of silence, the insistence of
his extended neck, his head bowing
to trumpet, almost a nod, almost
gentlemanly as I walk past
towards the mailbox. Each day,
familiar, there is this shadow, the grace
of his red bill open in acknowledgement.

POSSESSION

Morning brings no baby
drumming a spoon on the empty
Quaker Oats box,
making that hollow sound.
Sun rises, barely, through gray.
My husband drives to work.
In bed last night, brooding hotly,
he said *Possession*
is not nine-tenths of love.
If it was, I wouldn't feel so bad.
His words puffed
into the dark room like steam
punching through the thick surface
of cooking grits.
I cannot know what he meant.
I think of what we own,
what we can afford.
Hidden beneath the car's back seat
a fist-sized pocket of rust
pushes up, threatens
to come through.
Belts need tightening,
screech out their complaint
with every right turn. The heater whines
as though there's something stuck:
a beetle, a leaf left over from autumn?
He's looked for it, but can't seem
to find or clear it out.
I hang laundry in the basement,
slip my body
into the rough-dry stiffness

of a dress. The day wears on;
the wrinkles never fall.
The house smells like split-pea soup,
fresh bread when he gets home.
You're a good woman he says.
Later, in the dark, he pulls
the dress over my head, drops it
on the floor. Like firefly-light
the static crackles.

RED WHOREHOUSE SOFA

If I stuck my tongue into these old grooves
the furrowed wood of the red whorehouse sofa
I might find a splinter and fill my mouth
with the taste of blood and old dust
It curves scoliotic   sags like a shoulder   I follow
its lines   a lumpy terrain   the almost rust-grained
nap of velvet   It hides rips held together
with safety pins   like the worn gown
of   an old woman who refuses mirrors
whose seam split   a slit run too high   revealing
pale varicose thigh
It keeps the smells of marrow   the memory of fire
and dead wood   I could strip it   find it animal
a skeletal patchwork of horse-hair stuffed boards
its black iron lion's paw feet screwed deep
into its splayed legs   In my lust for texture
I am afraid to leave its broken lap
It offers a layered history of lives I slip
into like shadow   familiar as family
I have built my living room around the beauty
of its battered curves   the creak of its belly when I twist
or turn   its bawdy sinking   the thought of recovering it

11:11 A.M.

The flashing red sign swings out
from the side of a school bus.
Three sets of distance separate you
from the boy looking down
from his seat. He can't hear
your car's heater wheezing.
You can't hear the little girls
giggling in the seat behind him,
their heads together as they
flip you the finger.
Your window's
rolled up to keep out
October chill.

The first tree to change
stopped you
again in the bathroom this morning.
Weeks you watched it turn:
yellow, then fiery; brown too soon.
Water running through copper pipes
heating the house
drowned out the sound
of the creek below.

You are waiting for the light to change.
This moment catches you
in your car. Be good, you tell yourself.
Don't waste this wish.

HELEN

> The most fascinating thing about Helen was her story.
> It was far better than she was.
>
> Robert E. Bell, *Women of Classical Mythology:*
> *A Biographical Dictionary*

This is what I know about me:
on sunny days I fall in love
with my own shadow,
her bouncy gait, the way
she stretches off from me
at that sexy forty-five-degree angle.
She exposes the way that someone real
can disappear in broad day-
light. Ecliptic, she moves,
all form, no features,
seductive paraphrase,
isogloss of woman
projected against concrete.
Some days I search the mirror
hungry for her flatness,
her unfilled edges.
I turn on all the lights,
position the medicine
cabinets to surround myself
in fifteen-layered reflection.
Sometimes I spot her:
the ninth me on the left;
the head that turned too slow,
periphery out of sync
with those other pleading-
eyed clones. She scrutinizes
me until I push her into
the chimera of myself
with the magnetized doors,

look away from myself in
her exasperated stare—
*Girl, you're looking
right through me*—
the words behind her
wide black eyes.

ACKNOWLEDGMENTS

The author gratefully acknowledges the editors of the following publications, in which some of the poems herein first appeared, some in slightly different form:

African American Review: "Leda," "Daphne," "Groove," "Danae," "Tamar's Blues"; *Callaloo*: "Red Whorehouse Sofa"; *Columbia*: "Incubus"; *Crab Orchard Review*: "Hum," "Bop: A Whistling Woman," "Magnificat"; *Rattapallax*: "Spring Bop: New York, 1999"; *Shenandoah*: "199 Lee Street." "Strip" first appeared in *Bum Rush the Page* (Random House). "Eight" and "Period" first appeared in *Role Call: A Generational Anthology of Social and Political Black Literature & Art* (Third World Press).

I am especially grateful for a generous grant from the Money for Women/Barbara Deming Memorial Fund. Thanks also to God, for every good and perfect gift, to my family, to friends/fellow poets, especially Lisa Parker, Honoree Jeffers, and Robin Puskas, who read these poems in progress, and to my husband.

LYRAE VAN CLIEF-STEFANON received her B.A. from Washington and Lee University and her M.F.A. degree from Penn State. A semifinalist in the "Discovery"/*The Nation* prize in 1999 and 2001 and a recipient of an Academy of American Poets prize, Van Clief-Stefanon has also been awarded a grant from the Money for Women/Barbara Deming Memorial Fund. She assisted Susan K. Harris in editing the new Riverside Editions *Adventures of Huckleberry Finn* (Houghton Mifflin, 1999) and is currently at work on her next volume of poems. She lives in Virginia with her husband, Justin, where she teaches English.